FAMILY LAW AND PRACTICE

LAW ON COHABITATION

QUESTIONS AND SUGGESTED ANSWERS

Written by Steve J Norton

LLB, GDL, MA (Industrial Relations & Employment Law), MRES (Law Research), LPC

Copyright © Stephen Norton 2020

All rights reserved.

ISBN-13: 9781660101573

The right of Stephen Norton to be identified as the author of this work has been asserted by him in accordance with the Copyright, Designs and Patents Act 1988.

All rights reserved. No part of this publication may be reproduced, stored in the retrieval system, or transmitted, in any form or by any means (electronic, mechanical, photocopying, recording or otherwise), without the prior written permission of the author.

Dedicated to Barbara and Leah

Acknowledgements

I have drawn on a number of sources in compiling the questions and answers for this book. I have looked at some past exam materials and my LPC notes to create my own problem question scenarios in the final chapter of the book. I have also looked at the Chartered Institute of Legal Executives (CILEX) materials for ideas. LPC CLP guide on Family Law and Practice is a useful source on practical application and procedure (referenced in earlier guides in this series).

Introduction

I wrote this guide book as I found the subject of family law and practice very interesting when I studied it as an elective on the Legal Practice Course (LPC). I did not study this subject academically as I studied different electives in my undergraduate and post-graduate legal studies but having grown older and become a husband and a parent (slightly later in life), family law and practice seemed to become more relevant based on my own experiences. I hope those studying this area of law, and anyone else interested in how family law and practice applies in practical situations find the question and answer format useful. They are aimed at the practical application of family law rather than any attempt at academic discussion or analysis, for those starting legal practice courses. I have used a number of practical questions and suggested answers and included a few examination problem scenario questions in the final chapter, similar to those found on legal practice courses.

I have broken up the different elements into manageable chunks in shortish guides following the syllabus of courses like the LPC.

I hope you find these guides useful for your studies or anyone else who may be interested in learning about some of the practical steps involved in different areas of family law. In this guide I deal with the subject area of couples cohabiting. The Guardian in an article last year(2019)[i] pointed out that the overall number of families in the UK rose by 8% between 2008 and 2018, from 17.7 million to 19.1 million. Government legislation on protecting cohabitees could be seen as lagging behind married couples and those in civil partnerships (which now includes both same and mixed-sex couples) at the point of breakdown of their relationship. This question and answer guide deals with the legal situation as it currently stands. It should provide sufficient information for those sitting exams/assessments or who just want a general understanding of the law in this area in a question and answer format.

CONTENTS

CHAPTER 1

Cohabitation - General outline of the law

General questions and suggested answers

CHAPTER 2

Disputes over property and Trusts

General questions and suggested answers

General questions and suggested answers

CHAPTER 3

Cohabitation contracts

CHAPTER 4

Law reform

Questions and suggested answers

CHAPTER 5

Cohabitation - Problem question scenarios

Questions and suggested answers

CHAPTER 1

Cohabitation - General outline of the law

General questions and suggested answers

Question

What is the general law governing cohabitation?

Suggested answer

The law on cohabitation is limited and piecemeal. There is little in the way of property rights guaranteed in statute law. Certain terms my be agreed between the parties, or applied by the courts based on legal or equitable rights.

Question

What kind of property rights are there for cohabitees?

Suggested answer

A couple may reach a written agreed such as a Cohabitation agreement (sometimes known as a Living Together Agreement) binding only if created as a formal deed (discussed in more detail in Chapter 3) agreeing terms on property distribution and other matters if their relationship ends. If no such agreement exists it may be left to the courts to reach decisions on any beneficial interests based on the facts of each case (discussed in more detail in Chapter 2).

Question

Is a "common law marriage" the same as a formal marriage or civil partnership?

Suggested answer

No. The term often used of "common law spouses" is misleading. In England and Wales cohabitants do have some protection in certain areas but cohabitation gives no general legal status to a couple. Couples in marriages or civil partnerships have benefit from certain legal rights and responsibilities[ii].

Question

What legal rights do cohabitees have?

Suggested answer

Cohabiting couples do benefit, generally in a similar way to married couples from the protection available under Part IV of the Family Law Act 1996 (FLA 1996) in terms of being subjected to domestic violence. Those sharing a home or who have previously shared a home can apply for non-molestation orders and/or court orders to regulate who occupies the home. This was extended by the Domestic Violence Crime and Victims Act 2004 (DVCVA 2004) to allow couples who had never cohabited to apply for non-molestation orders (and strengthened the status of same-sex partners in particular concerning occupation orders).

In 2015 a new offence of "coercive control" was introduced through section 76 of the Serious Crime Act 2015 (SCA 2015). This applied to people in "intimate personal relationships", or where they live together, and have been in an intimate personal relationship, or are in "the same family". Family in this context includes "spouses", "ex-spouses", "civil partners", "ex civil partners" and people who have a child together. The Domestic Abuse Bill 2017-2019 if passed in Parliament, would keep protection for people "personally connected to each other" which includes people in "intimate personal relationships".[iii]

Question

Are there other areas of legal protection for cohabitees?

Suggested answer

The protections are mainly through common law and equitable principles referred to in the first question through written agreements (signed as deeds) and beneficial interests (trusts). These will be covered in more detail in later chapters.

Question

What other legal rights do cohabitees not benefit from or need to meet additional requirements?

Suggested answer

There are several.

(i) Inheritance – Where a couple live together and are not married or in a civil partnership, and one of them dies without leaving a will, the survivor has no right under the intestacy rules to inherit part of his/her estate.

(ii) Welfare benefits -The unit of claim for means-tested benefits and Universal Credit is the "family". This includes the claimant and their husband, wife or civil partner, or someone they live with *as if they were* husband, wife or civil partner. This also applies to many other current benefits (in a state of flux) such as income-based Job Seekers Allowance (JSA) as well as contributory benefits (based on National Insurance (NI) payments received rather than income). The Department for Work and Pensions (DWP) have no powers to recover benefits from any cohabitee not married or in a civil partnership. In terms of contributory benefits couples not married or in a partnership will lose their right to bereavement benefits if they start living together as if they were married. The latest benefit introduced in 2017 (Bereavement Support Allowance) replaced previous benefits but did not extend to unmarried couples.

(iii) Pensions – State pensions – A cohabitee cannot rely on their former partner's contributions for the purposes of state pensions.

(iv) Taxation – For taxation purposes cohabiting couples are treated as unconnected individuals and cannot benefit, for example, from various reliefs and exemptions in the taxation system that are available for spouses and civil partners.

(v) Registration of birth by parent – If parents of a child are not married, the father's details may only be recorded if both parents, or the court, recognise the father's paternity. For the father's details to be entered on the register this must be in the following circumstances:-

- The mother and father sign the birth register together, or

- One parent completes a statutory declaration of parentage form and the other takes the signed form to register the birth,
- One parent goes to register the birth with a document from the court (i.e. a court order) giving the father parental responsibility.

NOTE: There is a useful summary of the legal rights of cohabiting couples provided by STEP [iv].

CHAPTER 2

Disputes over property and Trusts

General questions and suggested answers

Question

What is the legal position regarding property when couples separate?

Suggested answer

When cohabiting couples separate the courts can only declare which person owns what. Most cases involve disputes over the ownership of the home. The legal owner of the land at common is usually the owner found in most cases at the Land Registry. If the land is unregistered this will be the last person the property was conveyed to. The sole legal owner may not however own all the equitable interest in the property. In land this may involve the creation of a trust. It may involve other kinds of trusts such as an implied trust, (i.e. resulting trust, or constructive trust) or proprietary estoppel. The courts will determine these issues.

Question

How are resulting trusts involved in determining ownership of land?

Suggested answer

A resulting trust is presumed to come about where A contributes to the purchase price of property that is in B's name, or A transfers property to B, not receiving anything in return. B is then seen as holding property on trust for A in both these situations. It may be possible to rebut this presumption if there is evidence that the parties did not intend to create a trust.

Resulting trusts can be established only by a direct contribution to the purchase price by the partner who is not the legal owner. *Curley v Parkes [2004]* [v] suggested that the contribution must be made at the time of purchase and that subsequent payments, such as mortgage payments, would not suffice. However, a direct contribution to the purchase price will not establish a trust if given by way of gift or loan. The successful claimant will be awarded a share to reflect the initial contribution made. Contrast this with the position under constructive trusts where, in the absence of any express agreement as to the size of the share, the court will decide what shares the parties intended by looking at the their whole course of conduct in relation to the property. *Stack v Dowden [2007]* [vi] suggests that, in domestic cases of cohabitants, resulting trusts are no longer the appropriate approach, and that these cases should be decided under the principle of constructive trusts. This was confirmed more recently in *Jones v Kernott [2011]* [vii].

Question

How is the concept of constructive trusts applied in determining ownership of land?

Suggested answer

For a constructive trust to arise the claimant must show there was a common intention to share ownership and that the claimant acted in reliance on this to his detriment.

The common intention can be established by an express agreement. In *H v M (Property: Beneficial Interest) [1992]* [viii], the parties lived together for 11 years, had two children, but never married. The assets included two bungalows in Essex and a property in Spain, all in the legal ownership of the man. The woman claimed a beneficial interest in the property. The court looked very closely at exactly what had been said by the parties as to how any assets would be divided. The man had said to the woman, 'Don't worry about the future because when we are married it will be half yours anyway and I'll always look after you and the boy'.

The man also made an excuse that the property was in his name alone for 'tax reasons'. As on the facts there was an express common intention (his statements to her), the woman had to show only that she had acted on this to her detriment. The court accepted that her detrimental action was the execution of a mortgage deed by her 'as occupier' postponing any rights she might have to the lender, thus prejudicing her domestic security. On this basis, the court awarded her an equal share in the English property, but dismissed her claim for a share of the Spanish house as no similar conversation had taken place.

The court will generally find a trust from discussions in the course of which the legal owner gives an excuse why legal ownership is not to be shared. In *Eves v Eves [1975]* [ix], a man told the woman that the property was only in his name as she was under 21 years of age.

Subsequently, she worked on various structural alterations to it. She was held to be entitled to a 25% share (see also *Grant v Edwards [1986]* [x]). However, in *Curran v Collins [2015]* [xi], the court said that such cases do not establish the proposition that the mere giving of a 'specious excuse' necessarily, or even usually, leads to an inference that, the person to whom the excuse is given can reasonably regard herself as having an immediate entitlement to an interest in the property in question.

If there is no evidence of an express agreement, a common intention to share the property can be inferred from the parties' conduct. Conduct such as payment of mortgage instalments and financial contributions to improvements to the property can be used to infer the common intention to share the property.

Contributions by labour may also count. In *Cooke v Head [1972]* [xii] the legal owner is bound to hold the property on trust for them both. This does not need to be evidenced in writing. Generally, <u>contributions to household expenses other than the mortgage</u> are much less likely to establish a trust. In *Burns v Burns [1984]* a wife was found not to have a beneficial interest in the property as it was the husband who had paid for the acquisition of the property and mortgage instalments. However in *Le Foe v Le Foe and Woolwich plc; Woolwich plc v Le Foe and Le Foe [2001]* [xiii], the court decided that it was entitled to infer that the parties commonly intended that the wife should have a beneficial interest as a result of her indirect contributions to the mortgage.
There must also be some detrimental reliance.

Working out the share. In *Jones v Kernott [2011]*, which was a case of jointly-owned property, the Court said that in situations where the property is in the sole name of one party, the first issue is to determine whether the other party has any beneficial interest in the property at all. If that is established then the court has to decide what that interest is. There is no presumption of joint beneficial ownership. The parties' common intention had to be deduced objectively from their conduct, but if this is not possible then the court will impute an intention to the parties, who will receive a share the court considers fair having regard to the whole course of dealing between them in relation to the property.

Question

How is Proprietary Estoppel applied in determining ownership of land on relationship breakdown?

Suggested answer

The doctrine of estoppel has been used to give rights of ownership: see *Pascoe v Turner [1979]* [xiv] (although remedies also include granting a licence to occupy or payment of money to the claimant, as in *Southwell v Blackburn [2014]* [xv]). Three elements are required:
(a) An assurance of an interest in the property;
(b) Reliance on that assurance;
(c) Detriment suffered as a result.
In addition, the above three elements must exist to the extent that it would be unconscionable to deny the claimant relief.

Proprietary estoppel is wider and more flexible than a constructive trust, which requires common intention to be shown rather than just an assurance.

If a non-legal owner does not have any beneficial interest in the property under the principles discussed above, he or she will have no right to remain there and may be excluded by the owner at any time on giving reasonable notice. However, in these circumstances the following ways of protecting the non-legal owner must be considered:
(a) Contractual licence;
(b) Licence by estoppel;
(c) FLA 1996, Pt IV;
(d) Childrens Act 1989 (CA), s 15 and Sch 1.

CHAPTER 3

Cohabitation contracts

General questions and suggested answers

Question

What is a cohabitation contract?

Suggested answer

An unmarried couple can draw up and sign a cohabitation contract which will set out what will happen to their property in the event their relationship breaks down. This will need to meet all the normal rules associated with a valid contract. In order to ensure they are legally enforceable unmarried couples are advised they take separate independent legal advice and write them as a formal deed.

Question

How do cohabitation contracts work in practice?

Suggested answer

A cohabiting couple will enter into an agreement setting out arrangements that will apply while they are living together, as well as establishing rights on the breakdown of the relationship. This is a developing area of the law and as yet there is no modern decision on the validity of such agreements. However, in *Sutton v Mischon De Reya and Gower & Co* [2003] [xvi], the court gave the strongest indication yet that there was nothing contrary to public policy in a cohabitation agreement. It is clear that solicitors are increasingly being asked to advise on and draft agreements in this field. The Law Commission, in its report, recommends legislation to make clear that cohabitation agreements are not contrary to public policy.

Matters to be covered in a cohabitation agreement

The main issues which could usefully be covered in a cohabitation agreement are as follows:
(a) Ownership of real and personal property;
(b) Finances, for example, how to divide bills and resolve ownership of joint accounts;
(c) Children, for example, their maintenance and surnames. Any agreement made in
relation to children will be limited by the CA 1989 and the CSA 1991 and will be open to
review by the court.
(d) Other matters: Here it is important not to include matters that are too trivial, or personal
matters, for example housework or division of chores, because this could make it more likely that a court would hold that the parties did not intend to create legal relations.
The Law Society has some basic guidance on

cohabitation agreements at https://www.lawsociety.org.uk/for-the-public/common-legal-issues/moving-in-together-getting-a-cohabitation-agreement/. Information on the rights of unmarried cohabiting couples is also summarized at https://www.lawsociety.org.uk/for-the-public/common-legal-issues/cohabitation-your-rights/.

Enforcement of cohabitation agreements

The general rules of contract will apply to the enforcement of cohabitation agreements. It might also be advisable to include an Arbitration Clause in the agreement for dealing with disputes between the parties. The Family Law Bar Association Conciliation Board's conciliation procedure is available to unmarried couples who have lived together.

CHAPTER 4

Law reform

General questions and suggested answers

Question

What attempts have been made to reform the law on cohabitation?

Suggested answer

In 2007 following consultation, the Law Commission published its report: <u>Cohabitation: the financial consequences of relationship breakdown</u> [xvii]. The report recommended the introduction of a new scheme of financial relief based on the contributions made to the relationship by the parties. It suggested the court should have the power to redistribute the ownership of the home when cohabiting couples separate. The reason behind this was to make sure one party does not suffer detriment due to any economic sacrifice they have made during the relationship (i.e. giving up their career to look after the children). Also, to prevent one party keeping any economic benefit made during the relationship.

A Bill was introduced via the House of Lords (<u>The Cohabitation Bill [HL] 2015</u>) but was defeated.

Question

Have there been recent attempts to reform the law on cohabitation?

Suggested answer

Yes, the Cohabitation Rights Bill [HL] was introduced via the House of Lords in 2017 and was due to receive its second reading in the House of Lords in March last year. In summary the contents of the Bill as outlined on the Parliament website are:-

The bill proposes to establish a framework of rights for cohabiting couples following the breakdown of the relationship or the death of one of the cohabitants.
The bill's provisions would apply only to those cohabiting couples who either had a dependent child or who had been living together as a couple for a minimum of three years. The bill would provide the right for either cohabitant, upon the breakdown of the relationship, to apply to a court for a financial settlement order to redress a financial benefit or an economic disadvantage resulting from the period of cohabitation. The bill would provide the right for cohabitants to opt-out of the financial settlement provisions, if they both agreed. In addition, the bill would provide

cohabitants with the right to succeed to their partner's estate under the intestacy rules and the right to have an insurable interest in the life of their partner, similar to the rights of married and civil partnered couples [xviii].

There is no further updates on the Parliament website on the progress of this Bill so it remains to be seen if it makes any further progress in 2020 under the newly elected Conservative government.

CHAPTER 5

Cohabitation – Problem solving scenarios

Questions and suggested answers

Problem question

Mary has come to you as a legal advisor to offer her some advice. She has been in a relationship with Harry for over a year now as an unmarried couple. They live together as a couple in a 2-storey house which they both own. She has heard there is some kind of contractual arrangement they could enter into to protect their interests. Can you advise her on this?

Suggested answer

Mary has informed you she is part of an unmarried couple cohabiting with her partner Harry in a house they both own. This means she cannot benefit from the same legal protections as a married couple particularly regarding property interests.

She has asked you specifically about cohabitation contracts. You can advise Mary she could draw up (or ask you to draft) a cohabitation contract which should set out what will happen to their property in the event her relationship with Harry breaks down. This type of contract will need to meet all the normal rules associated with a valid contract. In order to ensure it is legally enforceable her partner Harry would be advised to take separate independent legal advice and create the contract in the form of a formal deed. It must be pointed out to Mary that both should have entered into the contract freely and without duress. The cohabitation contract must include terms on their property and financial arrangements if they separate. It is important to pay great attention on any property owned. In Mary's case you will need to clarify how the property is owned (i.e. jointly as joint-tenants or as tenants-in-common where there may be a Declaration of Trust setting out percentage of ownership based on share of ownership in the property). These are matters that you need to draw out in any interview with Mary to ensure the contract reflects accurately her wishes.

Problem question

Sayed has come in to see you to offer him legal advice. He lives in a two-bedroomed house with his partner Faiza. He tells you they are not married or in a civil partnership. The House is in Faiza's sole name as she is the main earner working full time as a senior director in a major IT company on a high salary. Sayed works part time as a clerk for a small local insurance firm on a modest salary. Sayed is a keen DIY enthusiast after attending several courses on DIY skills. He has carried out some major internal refurbishment work on the property they both live in. He has re-wired the property, redesigned the kitchen, redecorated the whole house and carried out a loft conversion using his own savings. Faiza had promised Sayed she would `see him alright' if they sell the house and move. They have no children. Recently they have not been getting on and have decided to `call it a day' for their relationship together and go their separate ways. Faiza has sent emails to Sayed informing him he has no rights regarding the house or other property they own such as the house which is registered in her name. She is keen to sell the property to pay for a new house with the proceeds near to her sister in the country. Sayed does not want to agree to this and wants to know his rights. They have no cohabitation contract. Can you advise him?

Suggested answer

Your advice to Sayed would need to involve a discussion around legal and beneficial interests when it comes to any rights in the property as such, as a starting point. This is relevant as Faiza and Sayed have not entered into a cohabitation contract so there does not appear to be agreement on what happens to the property in the event their relationship comes to an end. As the house is in Faiza's sole name there is the presumption that she holds all of the beneficial interest in addition to being the legal owner as the property appears to be registered in her name at the Land Registry. This is one of the presumptions in *Stack v Dowden [2007]*. If the property was in both of their names, then it would be presumed that they share the beneficial interest equally. The upshot of this would be that Faiza owns the house both legally and beneficially, and Sayed would not be entitled to any share of the property.

This presumption however, is rebuttable. You should advise Sayed that he could attempt to rebut this presumption by arguing a trust has been established. There appears not to be any express trust agreed between them, but he may be able to show he has an interest under an implied trust. In order to establish this Sayed will have to use the test that was established under the case of *Lloyds Bank v Rosset [1990]* [xix]. He will need to show although Faiza was the legal and beneficial owner that there was a common intention between them that he would share an interest, and he acted to his detriment, or had made direct contributions to the purchase or value of the property. Sayed could argue the latter, as he used his own money to pay for major refurbishment of the house which could be argued increased the value of the property.

He would be advised to make an application under the Trusts of Land and Appointment of Trustees Act 1996 (TLATA 1996). He needs the court to make a declaration of his interest, and quantify it based on looking at the whole course of dealings between him and Faiza based on *Oxley v Hiscock* [2004] EWCA 546[xx]. The court may rule in Sayed's case that a constructive trust is appropriate and calculate his share based on his contribution in enhancing the value of the property based on Oxley. Under the TLATA 1996 Sayed would be advised to apply under S.14 to postpone the sale of the house. The court will apply the factors under S.15 listed below:-

Matters relevant in determining applications.

(1)The matters to which the court is to have regard in determining an application for an order under section 14 include—

(a) the intentions of the person or persons (if any) who created the trust,

(b) the purposes for which the property subject to the trust is held,

(c) the welfare of any minor who occupies or might reasonably be expected to occupy any land subject to the trust as his home, and

(d) the interests of any secured creditor of any beneficiary

In summary

- Advise Sayed he may have a strong case to show the existence of a beneficial interest in the form of a constructive trust.

- He should make an application under the TLATA 1996 for the court for a declaration of interest and to quantify his shares in the property and postpone any sale until this occurs. The court can make an order to this effect.

Problem question

Nadia has come to you for help and advice regarding her situation. She has lived with Andrew as an unmarried couple in a 3-bedroom house. The house was owned by

Andrew before he met Nadia, but when she moved into the property Andrew assured Nadia if their relationship came to an end, he agreed to divide the shares in the house equally, which he confirmed in an email to her. They did no put this in writing in any form of cohabitation contract. There is a small mortgage on the property in Andrew's name.

They have one son called David who was born in 2010 and is now 8 years old. Andrew is named on David's birth certificate as his father. Nadia works part time as a teaching assistant and contributes half of what she earns into a joint bank account, towards paying some of the mortgage and household bills resulting in some personal hardship to herself.

Nadia has discovered that Andrew has been texting another woman and when she confronted him about this and staying out late several times a week, he confessed to having and affair. She told him she no longer trusts him or wants to remain in a relationship with him and they decide to end their relationship.

Although they have been living together in the property until now, Andrew now wants to sell the house to move into a different area closer to his work. Nadia is afraid if Andrew sells the house she will get none of the proceeds as they had not agreed any formal written arrangements to divide up the property if the relationship ended.

Nadia is also concerned Andrew has different ideas regarding David. He has said he wants David to stay living with him in his new property once he moves in for the majority of the time. Nadia believes he should live with her and spend an equal amount of time with both parents which would be her preference as a fair outcome.

She has come to you for help and advice as she wants to know where she stands on her rights regarding the house and access to their son.

Suggested answer

When you offer advice to Nadia you will need to explain the law in a umber of areas as they apply to her situation. Firstly, you are told that there is no formal written agreement agreeing any terms on the division of their property on relationship breakdown. This means it is likely she will need to take action in court for them to determine her rights over the property. Secondly, you need to explain to her what procedures she would need to take to achieve the outcome she wants on access to their child and his upbringing.

Nadia has told you that Andrew owned the house which makes him the sole legal owner as well as having the beneficial interest when the house is sold. This on the face of it means Nadia has no rights in the property if the presumptions in *Jones v Kernott [2011]* and *Stack v Dowden [2007]* are applied. However, Nadia may be able to rebut these presumptions under the doctrine of implied trusts, either a resulting or constructive trust.

A resulting trust can only be established where a direct contribution to the purchase price by the partner has been made, who is not the legal owner. In *Curley v Parkes [2004]* it was suggested that the contribution must be made *at the time of the purchase* and that *subsequent payments such as mortgage payments* would not be sufficient. If applied to Nadia's situation, it is unlikely she could show there was a resulting trust as the house was already owned by Andrew when they decided to live together as cohabitees. The case of *Stack v Dowden [2007]* suggests that in cases involving cohabitees, resulting trusts are not the appropriate mechanism, instead constructive trusts are more appropriate.

A constructive trust requires that a person shows there was a *common intention* to share ownership and that the they acted in reliance on this to his/her detriment. There can be an express agreement *(H v M (Property: Beneficial Interest) [1992]*) where the legal owner had said to the woman that sometime in the future when they were married half of the property will be hers, and she had acted to her detriment. If applied to Nadia's situation, Andrew has agreed on the outset that if their relationship ended he would share the property equally with her. She could argue this constitutes an express agreement and she could show she has acted to her detriment paying towards the mortgage and household bills causing her financial hardship. In the absence of evidence of an express agreement, it may be possible for a common intention to be inferred from the parties' conduct. This would include payment of mortgage instalments and financial contributions to improvements to the property can be used to infer the common intention to share the property. Contributions to household expenses only are unlikely to be enough to establish a trust (*Burns v Burns [1984] Ch 317* [xxi]).

Nadia has contributed towards both the mortgage and household bills so that should strengthen her case in arguing the existence of a trust. Also in *Le Foe v Le Foe and Woolwich plc; Woolwich plc v Le Foe and Le foe [2001]* the court decided it was entitled to infer that the parties commonly intended that the wife should have a beneficial interest as a result of he indirect contributions to the mortgage (noting need for detriment). The Court of Appeal in *Ely v Robson [2016]* found a letter purporting to record a verbal agreement on beneficial interest made between separating couples was sufficient evidence of their intentions regarding the family home. The terms of the agreement in that case were seen as clear and comprehensive enough to form the basis of a binding agreement that one party/former partner (who was sole owner) held the property on trust for the other (until a specified event occurred when they would have to leave). Andrew has promised Nadia he will divide up the property equally with her and confirmed in an email which could meet the requirements for a constructive trust.

Nadia would need to apply to the court through an application under the TLATA 1996 for the court to make a declaration of interest, and quantify it through looking at the whole course of dealing between her and Andrew (*Oxley v Hiscock [2004]*). If she is successful her share would be held through a constructive trust. Under S.14 of TLATA 1996 she can apply to postpone the sale of the house, and the court will apply the factors that are listed under S.15.

The last issue Nadia has asked you to advise her on are her rights concern their son David. It seems from what Nadia has told you that David is their biological son and Andrew was named as the child's father. This means as per S.14 CA 1989 Andrew has parental responsibility for David as an unmarried father, as the child was born after 1

December 2003. Nadia having given birth to David has automatic parental responsibility. If as it appears, Andrew wants David to live with him Nadia can apply for a S.8 Child Arrangements Order (CA 1989 as amended by the Children and Families Act 2014 (CFA 2014)) for David to live with her and Andrew for equal periods of time (shared residence). The courts will apply the welfare/paramountcy principle and importance of both parents being involved in a child's upbringing. The relevant factors will be applied (i.e. children's wishes and feelings, age of child/children, educational needs, ability to cope with any change) It may be possible for Nadia and Andrew resolve this matter without a court order (collaborative law/ADR) which you could discuss with Nadia as a first option. If Nadia is able to establish a beneficial interest under a constructive trust to remain in the property for period she could argue stability, continuity, prevention of disruption in schooling etc. for David to remain living in the family home with her.

In summary

- Advise Nadia to argue the existence of a constructive trust where she has a beneficial interest.

- Seek a S.8 Child Arrangements Order to

arguing their son David she live with her relying on the relevant factors, possibly along the lines of the likely adverse effect a disruption caused by him moving home and area (friends, education etc). Contact could be agreed to determine contact with Andrew (how often he can see his son and visits to his home etc.).

- It is important you stress to Nadia the importance of seeking to reach agreement with Andrew without the need for attending court or issuing court orders wherever this can be done to resolve certain issues. This may be particularly important in child arrangements where their son David is concerned.

Table of cases

Burns v Burns [1984] Ch 317
Cooke v Head [1972] 1 WLR 518
Curley v Parkes [2004] EWCA Civ 1515
Curran v Collins [2015] EWCA Civ 404
Eves v Eves [1975] 1 WLR 1338
Grant v Edwards [1986] Ch 638
H v M (Property: Beneficial Interest) [1992] 1 FLR 229
Jones v Kernott [2011] UKSC 53
Le Foe v Le Foe and Woolwich plc; Woolwich plc v Le Foe and Le Foe [2001] 2 FLR 970
Lloyds Bank v Rosset [1990] UKHL 14
Oxley v Hiscock [2004] EWCA 546
Pascoe v Turner [1979] 1 WLR 431
Southwell v Blackburn [2014] EWCA Civ 1347
Stack v Dowden [2007] 2 AC 432
Sutton v Mischon De Reya and Gower & Co [2003] EWHC 3166 (Ch), [2004] 1 FLR 837

Table of Statutes/Bills

Children Act 1989
Child Support Act 1991
Domestic Violence Crime and Victims Act 2004
Family Law Act 1996
Children and families act 2014
Serious Crime Act 2015
Trusts of Land and Appointment of Trustees Act 1996

Cohabitation Rights Bill 2017-2020

ABOUT THE AUTHOR

I have studied law for many years as a part time student and have both undergraduate and post graduate qualifications and have completed the LPC. I have worked in voluntary paralegal/legal support roles. I worked as a civil servant for many years dealing with health policy as well as well as employment and collective bargaining procedures and complex personal case work. I maintain a keen interest in legal issues in particular, as well as other areas of study.

INDEX

Agreement, 9, 18, 19, 20, 25, 26, 27, 36, 41, 42, 43, 46

Beneficial owner, 37

Children, 6, 19, 26, 30, 36, 45

Cohabitation, 9, 10, 25, 26, 27, 29, 30, 31, 34, 36, 39, 51

Cohabitation contract, 25, 34, 36, 39

Constructive trust, 17, 18, 22, 38, 41, 42, 44, 45

Constructive trusts, 18, 42

Contract, 25, 27, 34

Domestic violence, 11, 48

Express trust, 37

Family, 1, 4, 5, 6

Financial, 20, 29, 31, 34, 43

Financial arrangements, 34

Home, 11, 16, 29, 39, 43, 45

House, 20, 33, 34, 35, 36, 37, 38, 39, 40, 41, 42, 44

Husband, 5

Implied trust, 17, 37

Individuals, 14

Law, 5, 6, 49

Legal, 5

Legal owner, 16, 17, 20, 22, 37, 41, 42

Owner, 16, 23, 43

Ownership, 16, 17, 18, 19, 20, 21, 22, 26, 29, 35, 42

Parent, 5, 27

Parental responsibility, 14, 44

Parents, 27

Resulting trust, 17, 41

Settlements, 6

Share, 18, 19, 20, 21, 35, 37, 38, 42, 44

Shares, 18, 39

Trusts, 7, 15, 38, 49

Unmarried couple, 25, 33, 34, 39

[i] https://www.theguardian.com/uk-news/2019/aug/07/cohabiting-couples-fastest-growing-family-type-ons

[ii] House of Commons Briefing Paper No: 03372 – 13.8.2019 "Common law marriage" and cohabitation

[iii] Ibid No:03372 – 13.8.2019

[iv] https://www.step.org/sites/default/files/Publications/cohabiting-couples-legal-rights-uk2.pdf

[v] Curley v Parkes [2004] EWCA Civ 1515

[vi] Stack v Dowden [2007] 2 AC 432

[vii] Jones v Kernott [2011] UKSC 53

[viii] H v M (Property: Beneficial Interest) [1992] 1 FLR 229

[ix] Eves v Eves [1975] 1 WLR 1338

[x] Grant v Edwards [1986] Ch 638

[xi] Curran v Collins [2015] EWCA Civ 404

[xii] Cooke v Head [1972] 1 WLR 518

[xiii] Le Foe v Le Foe and Woolwich plc; Woolwich plc v Le Foe and Le Foe [2001] 2 FLR 970

[xiv] Pascoe v Turner [1979] 1 WLR 431

[xv] Southwell v Blackburn [2014] EWCA Civ 1347

[xvi] Sutton v Mischon De Reya and Gower & Co [2003] EWHC 3166 (Ch), [2004] 1 FLR 837

[xvii] www.lawcom.gov.uk/app/uploads/2015/03/lc307_Cohabitation.pdf

[xviii] https://researchbriefings.parliament.uk/ResearchBriefing/Summary/LLN-2019-0030#fullreport

[xix] Lloyds Bank v Rosset [1990] UKHL 14

[xx] Oxley v Hiscock [2004] EWCA 546

[xxi] Burns v Burns [1984] Ch 317

www.ingramcontent.com/pod-product-compliance
Lightning Source LLC
Chambersburg PA
CBHW040328220526
45473CB00009B/2613